There Is a Country

BY

Matthew K. Cobb

TABLE OF CONTENTS

CHAPTER 1 4

INTRODUCTION 4

CHAPTER 2 9

THE GENESIS OF NATIONS...9

CHAPTER 3 14

DIVERSE LANDSCAPES 14

CHAPTER 4 18

CULTURAL TAPESTRY 18

CHAPTER 5 22

POLITICAL FRAMEWORK...22

CHAPTER 6 27

ECONOMIC LANDSCAPES 27

CHAPTER 7 32

SOCIAL DYNAMICS...32

CHAPTER 8 38

ENVIRONMENTAL PERSPECTIVES 38

CHAPTER 9..43

TECHNOLOGICAL ADVANCEMENTS.............................43

CHAPTER 10..**49**

CHALLENGES AND OPPORTUNITIES.............................49

CHAPTER 11...53

FUTURE OUTLOOK..53

CHAPTER 12..**57**

CONCLUSION 57

GLOSSARY OF TERMS..61

CHAPTER 1

INTRODUCTION

1.1 Definition and Overview

The notion of a country is as old as human civilization itself, yet its significance and complexity continue to grow over time. A nation, in its simplest definition, refers to a separate geographical territory administered by a sovereign government. However, underlying this easy explanation is a complex tapestry of history, culture, politics, economy, and social dynamics that form the character and fate of any nation.

At its essence, a country symbolizes more than just a landmass outlined by boundaries on a map. It embodies the collective goals, challenges, successes, and common identity of its people. From the ancient civilizations of Mesopotamia and Egypt to the modern-day nation-states that dot the world landscape, the notion of a country has experienced a remarkable transformation, reflecting the shifting dynamics of human society.

Throughout history, countries have evolved through numerous tactics, including conquest, colonialism, revolution, and peaceful negotiation. These processes have impacted the geopolitical environment, frequently leaving a permanent mark on the cultural, linguistic, and political composition of nations. The borders that define countries are not only lines on a map; they designate the geographical sovereignty within which a nation exercises its authority and expresses its identity.

1.2 Significance of Exploring Countries

The study of countries bears tremendous relevance in understanding the intricacies of our globe. By diving into the subtleties of other nations, we obtain insights into the varied array of human experiences, viewpoints, and issues. Each country boasts its own unique blend of history, culture, geography, and socio-political dynamics, making it a fascinating subject of investigation and analysis.

One of the key motivations for traveling to nations is to build a greater understanding of cultural variety. Every nation claims its own collection of customs, traditions, dialects, and creative manifestations, which serve as the building blocks of its cultural identity. By immersing ourselves in the rich tapestry of different cultures, we build empathy, tolerance, and cross-cultural understanding, crucial values in an increasingly linked world.

Moreover, the study of countries helps us to appreciate the complexity of governance and political systems. From democracies to authoritarian regimes, each nation chooses a distinctive style of governance, driven by historical legacies, ideological views, and socio-economic considerations. By studying the strengths and limitations of diverse political frameworks, we may garner vital insights into the concepts of democracy, human rights, and the rule of law.

Furthermore, exploring nations gives information on the economic forces that drive global prosperity and inequality. From industrial powerhouses to agricultural cultures, each nation contributes to the global economy in its own manner, affecting trade, investment, and development patterns. By understanding the elements that support economic growth and creativity, we may uncover possibilities for cooperation, innovation, and equitable development.

In addition, the study of countries helps us to engage with significant global concerns, such as climate change, pandemics, poverty, and violence. While these concerns transcend national boundaries, they often emerge in unique ways inside various countries, demanding personalized responses and joint efforts. By understanding the core causes and implications of these difficulties within unique country settings, we may create more effective policies for mitigation and resilience-building.

In short, visiting countries gives a window into the varied character of our planet, demonstrating the interconnection of societies, cultures, and ecosystems beyond boundaries. By digging into the rich tapestry of human experiences and ambitions, we get a greater respect for the diversity, resilience, and promise of nations throughout the globe. As we start on this voyage of discovery, let us embrace the intricacies of our world with curiosity, humility, and dedication to create a more fair, equitable, and sustainable future for everyone.

CHAPTER 2
THE GENESIS OF NATIONS

2.1 Historical Perspective

The birth of countries is a tapestry woven with threads of history, politics, and human endeavor. To comprehend the origin of countries, we must dive into the annals of time when civilizations grew and fell, boundaries altered, and identities emerged.

Throughout history, the definition of a country has evolved, molded by conquests, migrations, and revolutions. Ancient civilizations such as Mesopotamia, Egypt, and China set the framework for the development of nation-states. These early communities created central governments, legal systems, and cultural identities, establishing the framework for the contemporary nation-state.

The Middle Ages witnessed the advent of feudalism in Europe when authority was dispersed among lords and monarchs. Kingdoms and principalities formed, each with its own customs, laws, and languages. The Treaty of Westphalia in 1648 represented a critical point in the history of countries since it established the idea of state sovereignty and set the framework for the current nation-state system.

The period of discovery and colonialism further changed the world map, as European nations carved out colonies around the globe. The legacy of colonialism is still obvious today, as many nations cope with the effects of past exploitation and tyranny. Decolonization movements in the 20th century led to the establishment of new states in Africa, Asia, and the Americas, as formerly colonial peoples claimed their right to self-determination.

The 20th century was distinguished by two global wars and the growth of nationalism, as countries attempted to establish their independence and sovereignty. The aftermath of World War II saw the foundation of the United States, aimed at encouraging peace and cooperation among states. The Cold War split the world into opposing blocs led by the United States and the

Soviet Union, influencing the geopolitical landscape for decades to come.

In recent years, globalization has broken conventional boundaries, as nations become increasingly integrated through commerce, technology, and communication. Transnational concerns such as climate change, terrorism, and pandemics necessitate a coordinated global response, undermining the concept of sovereignty in a linked world.

2.2 Evolution of Borders and Boundaries

Borders are not only lines on a map; they are symbols of identity, sovereignty, and power. Throughout history, boundaries have altered as empires grew and fell, wars were conducted, and treaties were formed. The notion of territorial sovereignty arose in the early modern period when nations strove to exercise control over their boundaries and defend their territory from foreign threats.

The creation of boundaries is typically a difficult process, as it entails defining the rights and obligations of governments and determining the destiny of ethnic and cultural groups. The partition of India in 1947, for example, resulted in the displacement and murder of millions of people as the newly formed nations of India and Pakistan fought to define their borders along religious lines.

Borders are not static; they are liable to change throughout time as a result of political, social, and economic causes. The dissolution of the Soviet Union in 1991 led to the establishment of new states throughout Eastern Europe and Central Asia, as former republics declared their independence and sovereignty. The disintegration of Yugoslavia in the 1990s resulted in the establishment of many new republics, as ethnic and nationalist tensions boiled over into violence.

In the 21st century, technological breakthroughs have made borders more porous than ever before, as people, products, and information move freely across national boundaries. However, this connection has also led to new difficulties, such as transnational crime, terrorism, and illegal migration. The growth of populist and nationalist forces in many nations has led to calls for stronger border restrictions and a reassertion of national sovereignty.

Despite the obstacles they provide, borders are also emblems of diversity and resilience, since they symbolize the diverse fabric of cultures, languages, and traditions that constitute the human experience. In an increasingly globalized world, the problem is in achieving a balance between the necessity to safeguard national sovereignty and the requirement to develop collaboration and understanding among states.

CHAPTER 3
DIVERSE LANDSCAPES

The landscapes of our globe are as varied and diverse as the people who live in them. From towering mountains to broad plains, and lush forests to expansive deserts, the Earth's topography impacts the cultures, economics, and history of nations around the globe. In this chapter, we dig into the vast fabric of landscapes that make up our world and investigate their tremendous effect on human cultures.

3.1 Geography and Topography

Geography is not only a question of physical characteristics; it involves a plethora of aspects that contribute to the particular character of a place. Topography, climate, natural resources, and location all play essential roles in creating the identity and growth of a country.

Consider the hilly landscape of Nepal, home to some of the highest peaks on Earth, including Mount Everest. The rocky topography not only poses significant obstacles but also offers prospects for adventure tourism and hydropower development. Similarly, the low-lying Netherlands has reclaimed land from the sea via massive engineering efforts, transforming it into one of the world's most densely inhabited and economically wealthy nations.

Climate also exerts a tremendous impact on countries and their populations. The searing heat of the Sahara Desert dictates the lifestyles of people who stay inside its boundaries, while the cold temperatures of Antarctica render it unsuitable to all but the hardiest of explorers. From the lush jungles of the Amazon to the frigid tundra of Siberia, the Earth's different climates impact the way people live, work, and interact with their environment.

3.2 Impact on Culture and Development

The link between geography and culture is symbiotic, with one exerting a substantial impact on the other. The availability of resources, accessibility of trade routes, and vulnerability to natural calamities all impact the cultural practices and economic activities of a civilization.

In island nations like Japan and Indonesia, where arable land is rare and isolation is a continuous danger, agriculture and fishing have long been vital to the economy and way of life. As a result, many countries have created rich culinary traditions focused on rice, fish, and other locally derived resources. In contrast, nations with enormous swaths of fertile land, such as the United States and Brazil, have historically relied on large-scale agriculture to power their economy, leading to the growth of monoculture farming methods and the production of cash commodities for export.

Moreover, the physical constraints imposed by geography have traditionally defined the political boundaries of nations, leading to the establishment of unique cultural identities and geopolitical disputes. The Great Wall of China, for example, acted as both a defensive construction and a symbol of imperial authority, while the natural borders of the Himalayas have long separated the Indian subcontinent from the rest of Asia.

In conclusion, the different landscapes of our globe are not only a tribute to the forces of nature but also a reflection of the inventiveness, tenacity, and adaptation of human cultures. By understanding the intricate interaction of geography, culture, and development, we get insights into the difficulties and possibilities confronting countries throughout the world and the ways in which they continue to create our collective destiny.

CHAPTER 4
CULTURAL TAPESTRY

Culture is the essence of a nation, the invisible thread that runs through its past determines its identity and bonds its people together. In this chapter, we dig into the complex tapestry of cultural variety that characterizes countries throughout the world.

4.1 Language Diversity

Language, probably the most unique identifier of culture, is a strong force that impacts cognition, communication, and identity. Across the planet, there are dozens of languages, each expressing a unique background and viewpoint. From the tonal subtleties of Mandarin Chinese to the lyrical flow of Spanish, languages not only promote communication but also embody the collective wisdom, culture, and customs of a people.

Within a single country, linguistic variety may be astounding. Take India, for example, where over 19,500 languages and dialects are spoken, ranging from Hindi and Bengali to Tamil and Gujarati. Each language represents the vast mosaic of India's cultural terrain, with its regional variances and subtleties.

Language is not just a method of communication but also a reservoir of cultural legacy. It maintains tales, myths, and rituals passed down through generations, forming the collective memory of a culture. In many situations, languages are endangered, and threatened by globalization, urbanization, and the dominance of major languages. Efforts to conserve and revive endangered languages are critical for protecting cultural diversity and advancing linguistic rights.

4.2 Traditions and Customs

Beyond language, traditions, and practices create the fabric of a country's cultural identity. Whether it's the boisterous festivals of Carnival in Brazil, the serious procedures of Japanese tea ceremonies, or the colorful celebrations of Diwali in India, traditions represent the values, beliefs, and practices of a society.

These practices frequently function as anchors in a quickly changing environment, offering a sense of continuity and connection. They enhance social cohesiveness, build communal relationships, and reinforce cultural identity. Through rituals, ceremonies, and rites of passage, traditions celebrate key milestones in life, from birth and marriage to death and beyond.

Moreover, traditions are not static but dynamic, changing in response to social, economic, and environmental changes. They adapt to new situations while keeping their core, displaying the persistence and flexibility of culture.

However, traditions may also be a cause of friction, particularly when they collide with modern ideals or impinge upon individual rights. Balancing cultural preservation with societal change is a challenging endeavor, requiring care, conversation, and mutual respect.

In recent years, there has been a rising acknowledgment of the value of cultural variety and the necessity to protect intangible cultural assets. Initiatives such as UNESCO's Convention for the Safeguarding of the Intangible Cultural Heritage strive to safeguard and promote cultural expressions globally so that future generations can continue to cherish the rich tapestry of human creativity and heritage.

In conclusion, culture is the heart and soul of a nation, representing its history, values, and ambitions. Language, traditions, and rituals are the threads that link civilizations together, generating a sense of belonging and identity. By accepting cultural variety and protecting our shared past, we can develop a more inclusive and harmonious world for years to come.

CHAPTER 5
POLITICAL FRAMEWORK

Politics constitutes the backbone of each country, determining its government institutions, formulating its policies, and affecting its interactions on the world stage. In this chapter, we dig into the rich network of political systems that characterize nations across the world.

5.1 Governance Structures

Governance arrangements vary greatly between countries, ranging from democracies to authoritarian regimes, each with its distinct system of authority.

Democracies, such as the United States, India, and many European nations, are defined by elected representatives who rule on behalf of the people. These systems frequently incorporate checks and balances amongst branches of government to prevent the concentration of power in any one institution. Citizens often exercise their political rights through free and fair elections, promoting accountability and openness in governance.

On the other hand, authoritarian governments, like North Korea, China, and Saudi Arabia, centralize power in the hands of a single leader or governing elite. Political liberties are generally curtailed, criticism is suppressed, and resistance is punished with brutal reprisals. While authoritarian governments may promote stability and efficiency, they frequently lack the democratic virtues of participation and plurality.

Hybrid systems, seen in nations like Russia and Turkey, merge parts of democracy with authoritarianism, showing features of both regimes. These regimes may contain periodic elections and limited political liberties but also concentrated power and limits on opposition.

Furthermore, federal systems, such as those in the United States, Germany, and Brazil, share authority between a central government and regional or state governments. This decentralization provides for more autonomy and responsiveness to local demands but also requires coordination and collaboration across different levels of government.

5.2 Diplomacy and International Relations

Diplomacy has a key role in the international arena, influencing ties between countries, supporting peace, and resolving global concerns.

Bilateral diplomacy comprises exchanges between two nations when diplomats negotiate agreements, resolve disputes, and develop collaboration on subjects of mutual interest. These agreements might vary from economic deals and security alliances to cultural exchanges and environmental partnerships.

Multilateral diplomacy, done through international organizations such as the United Nations, NATO, and the European Union, includes collaboration between numerous countries to solve global challenges including climate change, terrorism, and human rights. These forums provide venues for conversation, negotiation, and collective action, combining resources and expertise to confront difficult issues that transcend national borders.

Soft power, a notion popularized by political scientist Joseph Nye, refers to the ability of governments to influence others by cultural, intellectual, and diplomatic methods, rather than coercion or force. Soft power tactics include diplomacy, cultural exchanges, international aid, and public diplomacy activities like broadcasting and cultural diplomacy. Countries like the United States, China, and France exploit their soft power assets to strengthen their worldwide influence and accomplish their foreign policy objectives.

In contrast, hard power depends on military and economic might to achieve strategic goals and project influence on the international stage. Major countries like the United States, Russia, and China possess strong military capabilities, including nuclear arsenals, and employ economic instruments such as sanctions and trade regulations to express their interests and deter prospective rivals.

Overall, political frameworks impact the conduct of countries in the international arena, influencing their foreign policy, alliances, and relations with other states.

Understanding these processes is vital for navigating the complexity of global politics and achieving peace, stability, and prosperity on a global scale.

CHAPTER 6
ECONOMIC LANDSCAPES

Economic landscapes create the base upon which nations develop their prosperity, altering the livelihoods of individuals and impacting global dynamics. From booming metropolises to rural hinterlands, every region of the world is distinguished by diverse economic activity that reflects historical legacies, natural endowments, and modern objectives. This chapter looks into the varied characteristics of economic landscapes, studying industries, sectors, and the subtle interaction of socioeconomic forces.

6.1 Industries and Economic Sector

Industries serve as the engines of economic progress, moving nations ahead via innovation, productivity, and trade. Across the world, numerous industries exist, each contributing distinctively to the broader economic environment. Manufacturing, long considered a cornerstone of industrial nations, comprises a spectrum of activities ranging from car manufacture to medicines. In rising economies, the industrial sector frequently sees fast development, spurred by investments in infrastructure and technology.

Moreover, the services sector has evolved as a significant force in the global economy, comprising a wide array of industries such as finance, tourism, and information technology. In industrialized economies, services generally form a considerable share of GDP, indicating the trend toward knowledge-based sectors and the rising importance of intangible assets.

Agriculture is a key industry in many nations, providing nutrition, employment, and raw materials for businesses. While technology breakthroughs have revolutionized agricultural methods, issues such as climate change, land degradation, and food security continue, underlining the need for sustainable agricultural growth.

6.2 Socioeconomic Factors

Economic landscapes are not just determined by the production and distribution of goods and services but are intricately connected with socioeconomic issues that affect the fabric of society. Income inequality, for instance, remains a chronic issue in many nations, sustaining differences in access to education, healthcare, and chances for upward mobility. Addressing income disparity involves numerous measures, including progressive taxes, social assistance programs, and inclusive economic policies.

Furthermore, the labor market dynamics play a significant role in constructing economic landscapes, affecting employment patterns, income levels, and skill needs. Technological improvements and globalization have led to shifts in labor demand, favoring high-skilled individuals in knowledge-intensive industries while marginalizing low-skilled workers in traditional sectors. Bridging the skills gap via education and vocational training is vital for encouraging equitable economic growth and lowering unemployment.

Socioeconomic stability is dependent upon solid financial systems that permit capital allocation, investment, and risk management. Banking institutions, capital markets, and regulatory frameworks constitute the backbone of financial ecosystems, enabling firms to get money, people to amass savings, and governments to finance public initiatives. However, financial systems are prone to systemic hazards, as illustrated by the global financial crisis of 2008, underscoring the significance of careful regulation and risk management techniques.

Moreover, access to essential utilities such as clean water, sanitation, and healthcare dramatically affects human growth and productivity. Improving infrastructure and public services is vital for raising living standards and encouraging economic success, particularly in emerging nations where infrastructure gaps inhibit economic growth and social progress.

In conclusion, economic landscapes contain a multiplicity of industries, sectors, and social elements that collectively influence the wealth and well-being of nations. By understanding the dynamics of economic landscapes and tackling significant obstacles, policymakers may design a route toward inclusive and sustainable development, ensuring that the benefits of economic growth are evenly spread across society.

CHAPTER 7
SOCIAL DYNAMICS

In the rich tapestry of human civilizations, social dynamics play a key role in molding the fabric of nations. This chapter dives into the varied facets of social dynamics inside countries, studying population demographics, social structures, and the issues and solutions that occur.

7.1 Population Demographics

The demographic makeup of a country comprises different aspects such as age distribution, gender balance, ethnicity, and urban-rural split. These demographics are not static but fluctuate over time owing to variables including birth rates, mortality rates, migration patterns, and government policies.

Age demographics give insights into the future workforce, healthcare demands, and pension systems. Countries with aging populations confront issues in sustaining economic output and offering appropriate healthcare services for the elderly. Conversely, nations with youthful populations may experience challenges linked to education, work prospects, and social integration.

Gender balance is another crucial part of demography. Disparities in gender equality can influence several aspects of society, including education, employment, political representation, and access to healthcare. Efforts to promote gender equality and empower women are crucial for ensuring sustainable development and social harmony.

Ethnic variety enriches the cultural landscape of countries but may also bring issues linked to social cohesion and integration. Managing ethnic tensions and cultivating intercultural conversation is crucial for establishing inclusive communities where variety is cherished rather than a cause of conflict.

The urban-rural split is a notable aspect of many nations, with metropolitan areas often displaying larger population densities and more economic prospects compared to rural parts. Addressing gaps in infrastructure, healthcare, education, and employment between urban and rural communities is vital for supporting equitable development and eliminating social inequality.

7.2 Social Challenges and Solutions

Despite advances in several facets of social development, countries continue to battle with a multiplicity of difficulties that undermine the well-being of their citizens. These difficulties include poverty, inequality, healthcare access, education gaps, prejudice, criminality, and social isolation.

Poverty is one of the most significant societal challenges internationally, affecting millions of individuals and families. Poverty not only deprives individuals of basic necessities such as food, shelter, and healthcare but also inhibits their possibilities for education, work, and social mobility. Addressing poverty involves comprehensive policies that incorporate economic empowerment, social protection programs, education, healthcare, and access to essential amenities.

Social inequality comprises gaps in income, wealth, education, healthcare, and opportunities that exist within societies. Widening wealth discrepancies can lead to social instability, damage faith in institutions, and impair economic progress. Efforts to minimize inequality may include progressive taxation, social welfare programs, investment in education and healthcare, and policies that encourage inclusive economic growth.

Access to healthcare is a fundamental human right, however, millions of people globally lack appropriate healthcare services. Improving healthcare access needs investments in healthcare infrastructure, training of healthcare professionals, expansion of health insurance coverage, and attempts to address healthcare inequities based on characteristics such as poverty, race, ethnicity, and location.

Education is a tremendous instrument for social mobility and economic development, however, millions of children throughout the world lack access to excellent education. Ensuring universal access to education, boosting the quality of education, and encouraging lifelong learning opportunities are crucial for developing inclusive communities and nurturing human growth.

Discrimination and social exclusion based on variables such as race, ethnicity, gender, religion, handicap, or sexual orientation remain common in many communities. Combatting prejudice needs legal measures, public awareness campaigns, and activities to promote diversity, tolerance, and respect for human rights.

Crime and violence pose substantial obstacles to social cohesiveness and public safety. Addressing the core causes of crime, such as poverty, inequality, unemployment, and social marginalization, is vital for reducing crime and increasing community safety. Strategies may include community policing, crime prevention initiatives, rehabilitation efforts, and tackling underlying social and economic causes that lead to crime.

In conclusion, recognizing and resolving social dynamics are vital for developing inclusive, egalitarian, and cohesive communities. By investing in social development, supporting human rights, and tackling systemic inequities, governments may create situations where all individuals have the chance to prosper and contribute to the well-being of society.

CHAPTER 8
ENVIRONMENTAL PERSPECTIVES

The environment is a crucial part of each country, affecting its scenery, influencing its culture, and providing resources for its population. This chapter dives into the environmental viewpoints of countries, investigating the wealth of natural resources, the issues of environmental deterioration, and the attempts toward conservation and sustainability.

8.1 Natural Resources

Countries offer different natural resources, ranging from mineral deposits and arable soils to extensive forests and freshwater reserves. These resources play a significant role in economic growth, providing raw materials for businesses, supporting agriculture, and powering energy production.

Mineral-rich nations like Australia, Brazil, and South Africa exploit their natural assets to generate economic expansion through mining and exports. Similarly, nations blessed with rich areas, such as the United States, China, and India, capitalize on agriculture to ensure food security and maintain livelihoods.

Forests represent another significant natural resource, giving timber, biodiversity, and ecosystem services. Countries like Canada, Russia, and Brazil retain huge wooded regions, which not only contribute to their economies but also function as carbon sinks, reducing climate change.

Moreover, freshwater supplies are crucial for maintaining life and supporting many sectors, including agriculture, industry, and urbanization. Nations like Canada, Brazil, and Russia are endowed with large freshwater supplies, whereas others confront issues of water shortage, such as those in desert regions or undergoing fast urbanization.

8.2 Environmental Conservation Efforts

Despite the wealth of natural resources, countries contend with environmental concerns originating from human activity, including deforestation, pollution, and climate change. Recognizing the gravity of these concerns, governments, organizations, and communities worldwide are pioneering conservation efforts to conserve the environment for future generations.

One of the key areas of attention is biodiversity conservation, aiming at conserving the diverse tapestry of life on Earth. Countries establish national parks, wildlife reserves, and protected areas to preserve essential ecosystems and safeguard endangered species. For instance, the Serengeti National Park in Tanzania and the Great Barrier Reef Marine Park in Australia are classic instances of conservation efforts focused on maintaining biodiversity.

Furthermore, attempts to mitigate climate change are gaining pace internationally, with governments pledging to decrease greenhouse gas emissions and switch to renewable energy sources. The Paris Agreement, ratified by virtually every government in the world, is a milestone commitment to limit global warming and mitigate its repercussions.

Additionally, sustainable resource management approaches are being encouraged to guarantee the appropriate exploitation of natural resources. This comprises measures such as sustainable forestry methods, water conservation initiatives, and eco-friendly agriculture techniques aimed at limiting environmental deterioration while serving human requirements.

Education and awareness-raising activities play a critical role in developing a culture of environmental care. By fostering environmental literacy and supporting sustainable lifestyles, governments allow individuals to make informed choices and contribute to conservation efforts at the individual and communal levels.

In conclusion, environmental attitudes differ greatly among countries, reflecting their distinct natural assets, socio-economic circumstances, and environmental issues. While some nations are blessed with bountiful natural resources, others confront serious environmental problems needing concerted conservation measures. By adopting sustainability principles, promoting collaboration, and empowering communities, governments can traverse the complicated environmental terrain and aim towards a more resilient and peaceful cohabitation with the natural world.

CHAPTER 9
TECHNOLOGICAL ADVANCEMENTS

In the current period, technical developments have become the cornerstone of prosperity and development for nations around the globe. From revolutions in communication to innovative inventions in many industries, technology has consistently transformed the landscape of countries, ushering in an era of unprecedented connection, efficiency, and opportunity. This chapter dives into the transformational potential of technology within the setting of nations, investigating its role in driving economic growth, and societal change and altering the future trajectory of countries globally.

9.1 Innovation and Technology Adoption

Innovation stands at the heart of technological development, leading civilizations ahead by pushing the frontiers of what is possible. Countries that promote innovation establish conditions conducive to creativity, research, and development, opening the path for innovative discoveries and innovations. From Silicon

Valley in the United States to tech hubs in China and India, innovation centers throughout the world act as catalysts for driving economic growth and global competitiveness.

The embrace of technology is another essential feature that separates forward-thinking nations. Embracing new technologies such as artificial intelligence, Blockchain, and the Internet of Things (IOT) allows governments to boost efficiency, simplify operations, and improve the quality of life for their population. Governments play a vital role in supporting technology adoption through supportive legislation, investment in digital infrastructure, and fostering collaboration between the public and private sectors.

9.2 Digital Transformation

The digital transformation has transformed the way nations function across numerous sectors, from government and healthcare to education and commerce. In an increasingly linked world, digitization has become synonymous with development, bringing new prospects for innovation and prosperity.

One area where digital transformation has had a tremendous influence is on governance and public services. E-government programs employ technology to increase openness, accessibility, and efficiency in government processes, enabling citizens to access services and information online effortlessly. Countries like Estonia have pioneered digital governance methods, creating a bar for others to follow in areas such as digital ID systems, e-voting, and digital signatures.

Furthermore, digital technology has altered the healthcare sector, bringing radical solutions for better patient care, diagnostics, and medical research. Telemedicine systems provide remote consultations and diagnosis, improving access to healthcare services in rural or disadvantaged locations. Additionally, modern data analytics and machine learning algorithms support individualized treatment plans and medication development, accelerating improvements in medical research and improving health outcomes.

Education is another subject witnessing substantial transition owing to technology. Digital learning platforms, online courses, and educational applications enable students access to quality educational resources anytime, anywhere. This democratization of education has the ability to overcome the gap in access to learning opportunities, allowing individuals to gain new skills and information regardless of their geographical location or financial level.

In the domain of commerce and industry, digital technologies have altered company structures, supply chains, and consumer experiences. E-commerce platforms have altered the way products and services are bought and sold, fuelling global trade and economic growth. Moreover, technologies such as 3D printing, robots, and automation are altering industrial processes, increasing efficiency, and allowing customized production at scale.

However, amidst the transformational potential of technology, it is vital to address the obstacles and dangers involved with digital transformation. Issues such as data privacy, cybersecurity concerns, and the digital divide underline the significance of responsible and inclusive technology usage. Countries must emphasize digital literacy efforts, cybersecurity measures, and legislative frameworks to guarantee that the advantages of technology are available to all while reducing any threats.

In conclusion, technical breakthroughs have emerged as a driving factor for prosperity and development in nations globally. By supporting innovation, embracing digital transformation, and tackling obstacles proactively, governments can harness the power of technology to unleash new possibilities, generate economic development, and improve the quality of life for their population in the digital age.

CHAPTER 10
CHALLENGES AND OPPORTUNITIES

In the complicated fabric of global geopolitics, countries confront a variety of obstacles while simultaneously being offered innumerable possibilities. This chapter digs into the varied nature of these problems and possibilities, analyzing the factors that influence the fate of nations in the contemporary world.

Global Issues Impacting Countries:

At the center of the current conversation are the important global concerns that transcend boundaries and impact countries globally. Climate change stands as a massive problem, affecting ecosystems, livelihoods, and whole communities. Rising sea levels, harsh weather events, and ecological degradation pose substantial hazards, encouraging governments to adopt sustainable policies and reduce environmental harm.

Furthermore, the prospect of pandemics remains large in the aftermath of recent global health disasters. The

COVID-19 epidemic underlined the interconnection of nations, illustrating how a health emergency in one corner of the world may fast snowball into a worldwide catastrophe. As such, governments wrestle with the requirement of improving healthcare systems, boosting pandemic preparation, and promoting international collaboration in disease control initiatives.

Economic instability poses yet another tough issue, exacerbated by circumstances such as trade disputes, market swings, and geopolitical conflicts. The interdependence of economies puts governments vulnerable to rippling effects emerging from distant coasts, demanding cautious fiscal policies, solid regulatory frameworks, and diverse economic strategies to weather the storm of uncertainty.

Moreover, socioeconomic gaps and inequality remain as enduring issues that weaken the fabric of societies. Income disparity, discrimination, and access to basic services remain controversial concerns, needing concerted efforts to promote social justice, inclusion, and equitable chances for all individuals.

Paths to Sustainable Development:

Amidst these problems, countries are given an assortment of chances to chart a road toward sustainable development and equitable prosperity. Embracing renewable energy sources offers a method for minimizing climate change while also supporting energy independence and stimulating economic growth. Investments in green technology, infrastructure, and sustainable practices have the potential to create employment, boost environmental resilience, and lowering carbon emissions.

Furthermore, the digital revolution brings unmatched prospects for creativity, networking, and economic empowerment. The advent of artificial intelligence, blockchain technology, and the Internet of Things (IOT) disrupt businesses, simplify procedures, and accelerate entrepreneurship. By utilizing the potential of digitization, governments may uncover new possibilities for economic diversification, boost productivity, and bridge the digital divide.

Additionally, encouraging international collaboration and diplomatic engagement is vital in resolving shared issues and embracing joint possibilities. Multilateral conferences, diplomatic dialogues, and cross-border collaborations serve as platforms for creating agreements, exchanging best practices, and mobilizing resources to handle global challenges effectively. By adopting a culture of collaboration and mutual respect, countries can traverse complicated geopolitical environments and establish a more safe, affluent world for future generations.

Conclusion:

In the broad tapestry of international relations, countries traverse a dynamic environment defined by a multiplicity of problems and possibilities. By facing global concerns head-on, stimulating innovation, and fostering collaboration, states may conquer hurdles and harness the potential for sustainable development and equitable prosperity. As we start on the road towards a brighter future, let us hear the call to action, paving a route towards a world where every country thrives, and every citizen grows.

CHAPTER 11
FUTURE OUTLOOK

In pondering the future of nations, one must travel through a maze of uncertainties and possibilities. The complexities of global geopolitics, technical breakthroughs, environmental difficulties, and socioeconomic transformations build a complicated canvas onto which the future of countries is drawn. This chapter digs into the different paths that nations could adopt in the future decades, studying emerging trends and the forces that will define their fates.

1. Emerging Trends

The 21st century has already witnessed the rise of various trends that are expected to impact the future of nations dramatically. One such trend is the growth of digitization and the Fourth Industrial Revolution. As technology continues to progress at an exponential speed, governments must adapt to embrace its promise properly. From artificial intelligence and automation to blockchain and quantum computing, the countries that lead in innovation and technology adoption are positioned to acquire a competitive edge in the global arena.

Another noteworthy trend is the increasing interconnectivity of the world through globalization and digital connectivity. This interdependence brings both possibilities and difficulties for states. On one hand, technology allows the interchange of ideas, commodities, and services, boosting economic growth and cultural interaction. On the other side, it exposes countries to vulnerabilities such as cyber-attacks, economic shocks, and pandemics, stressing the significance of collaboration and resilience in the face of adversity.

Furthermore, population transitions are changing the social fabric of nations. With aging populations in many affluent nations and youthful demographics in developing economies, governments must establish policies to manage the ramifications of these demographic shifts, including healthcare, education, and workforce development.

2. Shaping the Future of Nations

The future of nations will be affected by a multiplicity of elements, including political leadership, economic policy, technological innovation, and social ideals. Effective governance will play a critical role in navigating the complexity of the 21st century, enabling equitable growth, building social cohesion, and tackling major concerns like as climate change, inequality, and geopolitical conflicts.

Economic policies will also play a major role in shaping the fate of nations. In an era of fast technological change and globalization, governments must embrace forward-thinking policies that promote innovation, entrepreneurship, and sustainable development. Investments in education, infrastructure, and research and development will be crucial to fuel economic growth and boost competitiveness in the global arena.

Moreover, teamwork and diplomacy will be important in confronting transnational concerns that transcend boundaries, such as climate change, terrorism, and pandemics. Nations must work together through multilateral institutions and agreements to develop collective answers to these serious concerns, realizing that no country can solve them alone.

At the same time, governments must be alert in defending their sovereignty and national interests in an increasingly linked world. Balancing the benefits of globalization with the need to defend national security and cultural identity will need skillful diplomacy and strategic thinking.

3. Conclusion

As we peek into the future, the only certainty is ambiguity. The route ahead for nations is loaded with difficulties and opportunities, and the decisions we make now will define the world of tomorrow. By embracing innovation, promoting collaboration, and preserving common values, countries may chart a road toward a future that is affluent, inclusive, and sustainable. It is a future that we must collaboratively endeavor to develop, realizing that there is no limit to what we can do when we work together for the greater good.

CHAPTER 12
CONCLUSION

In the enormous fabric of mankind, countries stand as colorful threads, knitted together by history, culture, and the ambitions of their people. Through the prior chapters, we've gone on a journey exploring the various layers that compose countries, from their birth to their present-day complications. As we approach the finish of our inquiry, it becomes obvious that the notion of "There Is a Country" transcends simple geographical limits; it contains the core of human civilization itself.

12.1 Summary

Throughout this book, we've explored different factors that characterize countries. We've walked through the historical corridors, observing the growth of nations and the formation of their identities. From the rough landscapes of mountain ranges to the spreading plains and coastal coasts, geography has played a key influence in defining cultures, economics, and even political borders. Cultural variety has arisen as a cornerstone of human civilization, with languages, traditions, and customs painting distinct pictures of each country.

Examining the political frameworks, we've watched the complicated dance of power, diplomacy, and governance emerge. The economic landscapes, too, bring a diversity of opportunities and difficulties, as nations seek wealth while contending with concerns of inequality, poverty, and sustainable development. societal dynamics also add layers of complexity, with demographic upheavals, societal difficulties, and the drive for equality changing the fabric of civilizations.

In our research of countries, we've also turned our eyes toward the environment, acknowledging the delicate balance between human advancement and ecological sustainability. Technological developments have heralded new boundaries, giving answers to age-old issues while simultaneously presenting ethical and societal concerns.

12.2 Encouraging a Global Perspective

As we complete our tour, it's crucial to focus not just on the diversity and intricacies of individual nations but also on the connectivity that connects them together. In an increasingly globalized world, the destinies of nations are connected, and the issues we face—from climate change to pandemics—require collective action and collaboration.

Encouraging a global perspective involves overcoming limited national interests and embracing the universal humanity that links us all. It means realizing that the success of one nation is closely related to the well-being of others and that our diversity should be appreciated rather than feared. It means cultivating communication, understanding, and empathy across boundaries, realizing that the answers to our most pressing concerns can only be discovered through cooperation and solidarity.

As we look into the future, the journey of countries continues, molded by the currents of history, the ambitions of their people, and the difficulties of an ever-changing globe. It's a voyage laden with uncertainty, but one loaded with endless potential. By embracing our common humanity and working together towards a shared vision of peace, prosperity, and sustainability, we can ensure that the tale of "There Is a Country" is one of optimism, resilience, and togetherness.

In conclusion, let us remember that while countries may differ in their languages, customs, and philosophies, they are all part of the magnificent fabric of human civilization, each lending its distinctive hue to the canvas of history. In acknowledging this variety, let us also celebrate the common links that unite us and seek to construct a world where every country, every community, and every individual may develop and thrive.

Together, let us start on this journey with open hearts and minds, appreciating the beauty and complexity of the world in which we live, and striving towards a future when the ideal of "There Is a Country" is fulfilled for everyone.

GLOSSARY OF TERMS

1. Nation: A vast group of people connected by shared lineage, history, culture, or language, occupying a single nation or region.

2. Country: A nation with its own government, inhabiting a particular region.

3. Geography: The study of the physical aspects of the earth and its atmosphere, and of human activity as it affects and is impacted by them.

4. Topography: The organization of the natural and manmade physical elements of a place.

5. Culture: The practices, arts, social institutions, and achievements of a specific nation, people, or other social group.

6. Language: The process of human communication, either spoken or written, consisting of the use of words in an organized and customary way.

7. Traditions: The transfer of traditions or beliefs from generation to generation, or the reality of being handed on in this way.

8. Customs: A customary and commonly accepted manner of behaving or doing something that is peculiar to a particular culture, area, or time.

9. Governance: The activity or way of governing a state, corporation, etc.

10. Diplomacy: The profession, activity, or skill of managing international relations, generally by a country's representatives overseas.

11. International Relations: The study of the interactions between sovereign governments, as well as between international organizations, non-governmental organizations, and multinational enterprises.

12. Economics: The branch of knowledge concerned with the creation, consumption, and transfer of wealth.

13. Socioeconomic: Relating to or concerned with the interplay of social and economic variables.

14. Demographics: Statistical data pertaining to the population and certain groups within it.

15. Social Challenges: Problems or challenges that influence the operation of society, are frequently connected to concerns such as poverty, inequality, or prejudice.

16. Environmental Conservation: The conservation and preservation of natural resources and the environment.

17. Innovation: The introduction of new ideas, techniques, or goods.

18. Technology Adoption: The process by which people or groups embrace and employ new technology.

19. Digital Transformation: The integration of digital technology into all elements of an organization, radically changing how it runs and offers value to consumers.

20. Sustainable Development: Development that serves the requirements of the present without compromising the ability of future generations to satisfy their own needs.

This glossary gives a baseline grasp of essential terminology connected to the research and analysis of countries and nations. Whether diving into political systems, cultural traditions, economic landscapes, or environmental concerns, these concepts serve as crucial tools for appreciating the intricacies of our global world.